Blood & The Big Easy

True Events of The Axeman of New Orleans

Introduction

Serial killers and their horrific killing sprees have been terrorising mankind for centuries. However, with the growing connectedness of the world, the rise in education and lowering of illiteracy during the nineteenth and twentieth centuries, along with people's love for a solid murder mystery, it is quite unsurprising that serial killers came to be better known in recent times.

When you think of the famous unsolved serial killing, your mind automatically goes back to Jack the Ripper's Reign of Terror on London's east end White Chapel district in 1988, that took the lives of five women in a gruesome manner.

Jack the Ripper was an unseen mass murderer who operated in the poverty-stricken areas around Whitechapel in London's East End area during 1888. The brutal killer was referred to as Whitechapel Murderer and Leather Apron in both the criminal case files and the contemporary journalistic accounts. Jack the Ripper generally attacked female prostitutes who worked and lived across the slums of London's East End area.

He would cut their throats before inhumanely butchering their abdomens. His ability to remove internal organs from majority of his victims led investigators to propose that he was likely to possess some sort of surgical knowledge. In one of the occasions, a large portion of the human kidney from his murder victim was mailed to the police. Arduous and sometimes even inquisitive efforts were made to identify and catch the brutal murderer, but all the efforts went in vain. A massive public turmoil had risen against the London Police Commissioner and the home secretary for failing to catch the serial killer, thus, causing the police commissioner to resign later.

'Jack the Ripper' was a name that emerged from a letter by a person who claimed to be the serial killer and got circulated in the media.

One of the most commonly cited suspects include Montague Druitt, a barrister and teacher with an uncanny interest in surgery who was claimed to be eccentric. Druitt was held suspect due to an investigator Macnaughten, who investigated the killings by Ripper for Scotland Yard, provided a memorandum which became public. In the memo, the investigator claimed Druitt to be the ripper, who disappeared after the final murders and his dead body was discovered later. Nonetheless, there is no solid evidence of Druitt being the mass murderer of Whitechapel as he lived Blackheath and had no connection to Whitechapel.

The second suspect of being the mass murderer Ripper is Willian Henry Bury. He was first held suspect in 1889, because there was a huge similarity between his wife's murder and the canonical five victims. Though Bury was arrested and executed in Dundee, Scotland, he was living in Bow, close to Whitechapel during the killing spree of Jack the Ripper. If we consider the eleven unsolved killings that occurred between April 1888 and February 1891, then we find that Bury stayed in Bow from October 1887 to January 1889, which places him in that area around the time when the crimes took place. Moreover, it was reported that graffiti that read: "Jack Ripper is at the back of this door" and "Jack the ripper is in the cellar" was found on his Dundee flat. This graffiti lead some people to believe that Ellen had been murdered to stop her from identifying Bury as Ripper. Though did not plead guilty to murdering his wife, two days prior to his execution, he made a confession that he had indeed killed his wife and wrote a confession as well. The man confessed that he had throttled his wife Ellen during a heated row then tried to dismember her body for disposal but didn't continue out of fear. However, Bury did not mention being the Ripper at any point during the confession. And during the investigation, a detective was sent for interviewing Bury in Dundee wherein, he was not considered a likely suspect.

James Maybrick is another name that arises in the list of being Jack the Ripper suspects. However, Maybrick wasn't considered a suspect until over a century after his death. Especially, since he was a cotton merchant from Liverpool. A diary appeared in 1992 which took credit for the murders of the canonical five as well as the other two killings. Though a name hasn't been mentioned in it, numerous hints and references make it conspicuous that it was Maybrick's. Following that, a pocket watch was found in 1993 that had J.Maybrick scratched onto it along with the names of the Ripper victims and the words 'I am Jack'.

Since the diary and pocket watch were discovered, it is believed that his wife, Florence, had found that her husband was indeed the Ripper and decided to kill him to place an end to the series of killings. However, this is merely a rumor and there is no solid proof to aid the theory.

Joseph Barnett is one of the most significant suspects of being Jack the Ripper. Barnett lived with Mary Kelly, the last of the canonical five victims of the Ripper. He is reported to have been in love with Kelly and was sick and tired of her being a sex worker. Barnett felt that he could support her financially and he did so for a while till he lost his job in June 1888. Following that, Mary Kelly went back to the flesh trade. It is believed that Barnett attempted to scare Mary Kelly away from prostitution using the Ripper murders but failed to do so. Ten days prior to her death, Mary Kelly had a heated row with Barnett which led him to move out of the property. Later, Mary Kelly was discovered ruthlessly slain in her bed in a locked room. The murder was one of the most horrendous compared to the other canonical five killings and it was the only one that did not occur on the street. Furthermore, it was the last one which provides a clear explanation as to why the murders stopped after her death. Joseph Barnett's physical description as well as his appearance at the time of the murder also matches the various eye witness reports. Nevertheless, there is no solid evidence, just a strong motive for Barnett being Jack the Ripper and committing the killings and it is merely speculation.

Another popular suspect was Michael Ostrog who was a Russian criminal as well as a physician who had been thrown into a mental asylum due to his homicidal tendencies. Aaron Kosminski, another major suspect, was a Polish Jew and a resident of Whitechapel. He was infamous for having intense hostility towards women (especially sex workers) and had been sent to asylum few months after the last Ripper case. Till 2007, there was no strong evidence for suspecting Kosminski except for the suspicions of officers. However, a shawl bought at an auction in 2007 reignited the suspicion on Aaron Kosminski. That particular shawl is claimed to be the one that was discovered lying on the ground near the horribly mutilated body of one of the Ripper victims. Since then, it had been passed down by an officer's family and in 2007 it was sold at an auction to Russel Edwards. The shawl still possessed traces of blood. Edwards immediately contacted Dr Jari Louhelainen from John Moores University I Liverpool and after going through some tests, he formed a link between Kosminski and Eddowes' distant descendants.

Nevertheless, there no suspicion over Kosminski before 2007 as there no evidence that linked Kosminiski to the brutal Ripper killings previously. Moreover, when he was admitted to the asylum in 1891 he didn't seem to be a threat or danger to his fellow prisoners, which leads to the question whether the man possessed the violent tendencies shown by Jack the Ripper through his cold-blooded murders.

But still, the evidence from the shawl has been open to criticism and people claimed that the evidence wasn't solid enough to come to a conclusion and consider Aaron Kosminski as the brutal Jack the Ripper.

Various noteworthy Londoners of that time, such as the renowned physician, Sir Willian Gull and the famous painter Walter Sickert have faced speculations for being Jack the Ripper.

Massive newspaper coverage led to widespread and long-lasting worldwide infamy on the murderer and the legend strengthened. The London Police led an investigation into a series of over ten terrifying killings that took place in Spitalfields and Whitechapel between 1888 and 1891. Unfortunately, they were unable to link all of those murders to the killings of

1888. Five of those victims- Annie Chapman, Elizabeth Stride, Catherine Eddowes, Mary Jane Kelly and Mary Ann Nichols have been referred to as the 'canonical five' and their homicides between August and November 1888 are believed to be the most likely connected.

The corpse of Mary Ann Nichols was found at dawn on Friday 31st August 1888 in Buck's Row (known as Durward Street today), Whitechapel. She had last been noticed alive nearly an hour before her body was found by a woman named Emily Holland, with whom she had once shared a room at a common lodge in Thrawl Street, Spitalfields, while strolling in the direction of Whitechapel Road. Nichol's throat had been severed by two profound gashes, one of which totally severed all the tissue down to the vertebrae. Her privates had been jabbed more than once, and the lower portion of her belly had been partially torn open by a deep, spiky wound, that forced her bowels to stick out. Various other cuts made to both sides of her stomach were also made by the same blade; each of those injuries had been inflicted through a downward thrusting technique.

On Saturday 8 September 1888, the week following that brutal incident, the body of Annie Chapman was found at around 6 a.m. at the steps to the entrance of the backyard of 29 Hanbury Street, Spitalfields. Similar to Mary Ann Nichols's case, Chapman's throat had been severed by two intense gashes. Her belly had been carved out completely, with a portion of the flesh from her gut being set on her left shoulder and another portion of her skin and flesh along with the small intestines — being pulled and set over her right shoulder. Chapman's post-mortem report further disclosed that her uterus and various parts of her bladder and vagina had been removed as well.

During the investigation of Annie Chapman's killing, Elizabeth Long expressed witnessing Chapman standing outside 29 Hanbury Street at around 5:40 am, in the presence of a dark-haired man who wore a brown deer-stalker and a dark overcoat, and bore a "shabby-genteel" look. As per this female eyewitness, the fellow had asked Chapman the following question, "Will you?" to which Chapman had responded, "Yes."

Catherine Eddowes and Elizabeth Stride were both slain during the early hours of Sunday 30th September 1888. Stride's body had been found at around midnight in Dutfield's Yard, off Berner Street (known as Henriques Street today) in Whitechapel. She had been killed with a single clear-cut incision, nearly fifteen centimeters across her neck which had severed one of her neck's arteries as well as her trachea before closing underneath her right jaw. No further afflictions to her body were found which has led to uncertainty as to whether Stride's assassination was conducted by Jack the Ripper, or whether he was interrupted during the attack. Various eyewitnesses subsequently notified the police about seeing Stride in the presence of a man in or around Berner Street on the evening of 29th September and during the early hours of 30th September. However, each of them offered different explanations: some stated that her partner was fair while others claimed that he was dark; some expressed that he was scruffily dressed while others declared that he was well-dressed. Therefore, identifying the murderer turned out to be a highly strenuous task for the London Police Department.

Catherine Eddowes's body was discovered in a corner of Mitre Square in London, nearly three hours after the discovery of Elizabeth Stride's body. Her throat had been sliced from ear to ear and her gut had been peeled open by a long, profound, and jagged wound prior to her intestines being positioned over her right shoulder. Moreover, in this case, a section of her intestine had been completely removed and set between her left arm and body.

The beastly incapacitated and disemboweled body of Mary Jane Kelly was found lying on a mattress in the room where she resided at 13

Miller's Court, Dorset Street, Spitalfields, at 10:40 a.m. on Friday 9th November 1888. Her face had been mutilated beyond imagination with her throat severed down to the spine, and the waist nearly unloaded of all its organs. Her womb, kidneys, and one of her breasts had been shoved under her head. Moreover, the other internal organs from her body had been placed beside her foot near the bed, while parts of her belly and thighs had been kept upon a bedside table. However, the heart was missing from the crime scene.

The ashes found within the fireplace at 13 Miller's Court indicated that Kelly's killer had burned numerous flammable objects to lighten the area as he incapacitated her body.

Each of the canonical five killings had been committed in the dead of night. The murders were carried out on or close to a weekend, either at the end of a month or a week. The incapitations turned more and more severe as the series of slayings continued, excluding that of Stride, whose assailant may have been interrupted. Nichols was not missing any organs; Chapman's womb and parts of her bladder and privates were taken; Eddowes' womb and left kidney were unloaded, and her face was deformed, while Kelly's body was miserably decapitated with her face slashed from all directions and the tissue in her neck being severed to the bone, though the heart was the only body organ missing from this crime scene.

Historically, the idea that these five canonical murders were carried out by the same assailant has been procured from contemporary documents which link them together while excluding the others.

Few investigators have asserted that some of the killings were clearly the work of a single assailant, however, an unidentified more extensive number of assailants operating independently were responsible for the other crimes. Notable authors Donald Rumblow and Stewart P. Evans argued that the canonical five is a "Ripper myth" and that three cases of Nichols, Chapman, and Eddowes can be undoubtedly related to the same assailant, but that minor certainty exists as to whether Stride and Kelly were also slain by the same person. Contrarily, others believe that the six murders between Tabram and

Kelly were the work of a single murderer. Dr Percy Clark, an assistant to the examining pathologist George Bagster Phillips, connected just three of the murders and assumed that the others were executed by "weak-minded individuals'. Macnaghten hadn't joined the police force until the year after the killings, and his memo comprises profound factual blunders concerning potential suspects.

The brutal killings were left unsolved and the legends surrounding these horrific killings became nothing more than a blend of research and folklore. The killing spree of Jack the Ripper has gained massive infamy across the world and even today, nearly every person across the western world knows about this British serial killer and the series of beastly murders committed by the unidentified assailant who struck terror into the hearts of most women during that time.

But, not too many people think of a bizarre string of murders that took place around 30 years later in another country and city but the killer was just as mysterious.

In May 1919, a year when the torments of the First World War were coming to an end, and when the glamorous era of Jazz music was beginning to take off, the onslaught of a mass murderer sent shivers down the spines of the citizens of New Orleans, Lousiana.

New Orleans, a city in Lousiana, also known for giving birth to the Jazz music, was terrorised by a series of killings. For over a year between May 23, 1918–October 27, 1919 six people were murdered and another six attacked by an assailant called the Axeman whose main method was to break into people's homes by removing a panel on a back door with a chisel and attacked them with either an axe or straight razor or both, when he killed with an axe it often belonged to the victims themselves.

Robbery was ruled out by the investigators as a motivation for the crime as money or belongings left in plain sight remained in their respective places.

These crimes took place in a time of massive changes both societal and social it was only a few years after the first world war and the world was still feeling the horrors of that terrible conflict and America was also going through the Influenza epidemic that killed between 20 to 50 million people but it was also the rise of women's right to vote but also something else was making a large impact especially in New Orleans… Jazz.

Most of the ruthless axeman's targets were either Italian Americans or migrants from Italy, which forced many to think that the killings were ethnically motivated. Numerous media platforms overemphasized this element of the murders and even considered the involvement of the mafia in it despite the lack of solid evidence. Few crime analysts even implied that the slayings were linked to sex and that the killer was possibly a sadist mainly pursuing female targets. Two criminologists that went by Damon and Colin Wilson put forward that the Axeman slew male victims just when they occluded his endeavours to massacre females, backed by cases in which the woman of the home was slain but not the man. A less likely idea is that the assassin committed the killings in an insane endeavour to facilitate jazz music as denoted by a note ascribed to the murderer in which he said that he would spare the lives of those who played jazz in their homes.

Jazz will be an important part of this book because it was important to the killer as well since he gave the people a reprieve for one night if they played jazz in their homes he would spare their lives, was he a musician?

I am not trying to solve the case I am just both history and mystery buff and this feeds both my interests and the City of New Orleans holds a strange fascination as place of history and culture.

The mysterious axeman who appeared as a ghost and left without leaving a trail, was neither caught nor identified. Moreover, his crime spree came to a sudden halt as inexplicably as it started. The killer's identity continues to be a mystery till today, though numerous plausible identifications of different possibility have been put forward.

Condolences to the victims and their loved ones and may they rest in peace.

A Brief History of New Orleans

The history of New Orleans, Louisiana outlines the place's evolution from its discovery by the French people in the early eighteenth century through its years of Spanish rule, then shortly back to French control then being taken over by the US in the Louisiana Purchase at the start of the 19th century. During the 1812 war, the final major battle was the Battle of New Orleans in 1815, which led to the US winning. Throughout the early nineteen hundreds, New Orleans was the biggest harbour in the South of US, shipping majority of the country's cotton and various other materials to England and other parts of Europe. With New Orleans being the largest metropolis in the Southern region at the beginning of the Civil War of 1861, it became an early prey for taking over by the union forces.

With its affluent and distinct cultural and architectural genealogy, the city remains a significant place for music, traditions, as well as sporting events.

The area that was going to become the city of New Orleans was constructed around 2000 BC when the Mississippi River deposited slime forming the delta region. Prior to European rule, the settlement was occupied by Native Americans for over a thousand years.

The Missipian people constructed huge mounds and monuments in the area. Afterwards, Native Americans formed a portage between the main waters of Bayou St. John and the Mississippi River. The bayou streamed into Lake Pontchartrain. Thus, it evolved into a crucial trade route. According to Archaeological evidence, settlement here dated back to at least 500 A.D.

By the 17th century, French explorers, traders and fur trappers reached the area. And by the end of the decade, the French formed a cantonment called "Port Bayou St. Jean" close to the head of the bayou which was later known as the Faubourg St. John neighborhood. In addition to that, the French constructed a mini fort called St. Jean (known later as Old Spanish Fort) at the beginning of the bayou at the start of the 17th century.

In 1709, the land near the Bayou was offered to French settlers from Mobile, but most of the French people left the area within the next few years as they were unable to grow wheat in that supposedly barren land. These early European settlements are now within the limits of the city of New Orleans (also known as The Big Easy) although they predate the city's official founding.

In September 1722, a tremendous hurricane hit the city, and blew away most of the buildings and structures. Post this calamity, the administrators implemented the grid pattern suggested by Bienville but that had been largely ignored by the colonists earlier. You can still see the amazing grid plan today across the streets of the city's French Quarter.

Joseph and Catherine Maggia

On the night of 25th May 1918, Joseph Maggia and his wife Catherine were horribly slain by the ruthless serial killer known as the Axeman of New Orleans. The anonymous killer slit their necks with a sharpened razor and then smashed their heads with the axe owned by them. Catherine Maggia, who was nearly beheaded, died on the spot. Joseph Maggia, however, remained alive and was found by his brother when they heard his loud groans from inside his home.

Lousi Besumer and his mistress Harriet Lowe

At midnight of 27th June 1918, Louis Besumer along with his mistress Harriet Lowe were nearly assaulted to death. A guy who was delivering bread for Besumer's grocery shop witnessed the crime when the Italian owner failed to meet him outside and take the delivery. Besumer was horribly wounded but still sane. Harriet Lowe on the other hand, had been knocked unconscious. The Italian grocery owner later alleged that a man broke stealthily intruded his home and smashed him and Harriet with a small axe. The investigators found the small axe inside the bathtub. Besumer managed to recover but his mistress succumbed to her injuries and died on 1st May 1919.

Anna Schneider

On 5th August 1918, when Ed Schneider returned home from work at midnight, he discovered his wife who was 8-months pregnant, mercilessly beaten and lying in a pool of blood. She retained some consciousness and informed the police that the last thing she recalled was a figure towering over her while she slept. Later, the investigators found that the assailant made his way into their home through an unlocked window and struck her with a lamp. Anna delivered her daughter a few days following the incident.

Joseph Romano

On 10th August 1919, Joseph Romano was found slumped over in a pool of his blood by his two nieces. The girls, Mary and Pauline Bruno alleged to have seen a heavy-built black man run away after committing the crime. He donned a dark suit and a slouch hat. The man who struck Joseph seemed to have intruded their home through a chisel in the door panel. However, like the previous cases, there had been no burglary and the attack seemed to have been out of nowhere. Unfortunately, Joseph passed away two days later.

Cortimiglia Family

On the 10th of March, 1919, a man named Lorlando Jordano heard screams inside the house from across his grocery store. He rushed to discover the source of the commotion. When he entered, he discovered Rosie Cortimiglia standing across the doorway and bleeding atrociously from a head injury while her two-year-old daughter lay dead in her arms. While her husband Charles, lay with a horrible head wound on the ground. Both had been struck by a sharpened axe. The family was taken to a Charilty Hospital. Charles managed to recover and was discharged few days later.

However, his wife lost consciousness and was kept for longer in the hospital.

Steve Boca

An Italian Grocer named Steve Boca woke up suddenly on the 10th of August 1919 to find a dark figure towering above him. The intruder hit him continuously with an axe till he was unconscious. Steve managed to move outside his home and collapsed near his neighbour's house. He sustained the most horrific injuries to his head and his skull had been cracked open which showed his brain.

Sarah Lawman

The Axeman struck a nineteen-year-old teen named Sarah Lawman on September 3rd 1919. The teen lay unconscious and bled horribly from head to toe. Her teeth had been knocked away and her skull had been cracked open.

Nevertheless, the teenager survived in spite of those horrendous injuries. The weapon of attack was again found to be a small axe lying in her lawn.

Mike Pepitone

On the night of October 27th, 1919, Esther Pepitone, wife of Mike Pepitone heard screams erupting from her bedroom. She rushed onto the scene and found two men escaping while her husband lay dead on their bed. It was found that the man had been stuck eighteen times with an axe.

Chapter 1

Joseph & Catherine Maggio

It was May 23 1918 and Joseph Maggio; an Italian grocer and his wife Catherine were sleeping side by side in their home on the corner of Upperline and Magnolia Streets where they conducted a barroom and grocery. The Killer broke into the house via the back door by removing a door panel using a chisel. The intruder then proceeded to cut both Joseph's and Catherine's throats with a straight razor, Catherine's throat was so deeply cut she was almost decapitated but Joseph survived long enough to be found but died soon after.

The killer then used an axe that also belonged to the Maggio's to bash both their heads in before leaving maybe to hide the real cause of death he then changed out of his bloody clothing into clean clothes but left the bloody ones at the scene along with the axe and bloody straight razor was later found in a neighbour's lawn.

The couple were found by Joseph's brothers Jake and Andrew Maggio they found there brother still alive but shortly died of his wounds before the medical assistance could arrive burglary was ruled out because no valuables or money was taken.

The straight razor that was used to kill the couple belonged Andrew Maggio, the brother of the deceased who conducted a barber shop on Camp Street. His employee, Esteban Torres, told police that Maggio had removed the razor from his shop two days prior to the murder, explaining that he had wanted to have a nick honed from the blade.

Maggio, who lived in the adjoining apartment to his brother's residence, discovered his slain brother and sister-in-law roughly two hours after the gruesome attacks had occurred, upon hearing strange groaning noises through the wall. Maggio blamed his failure to hear any noise related to the attacks that had occurred in the early morning hours on his intoxicated state, as he had returned home after a night of celebration prior to his departure to join the navy; police, however, were nonetheless surprised that he failed to hear the intruder, as he made a forced entry into the home as he had returned home after a night of celebration prior to his departure to join the navy; police, however, were nonetheless surprised that he failed to hear the intruder, as he made a forced entry into the home.

Since the razor of the axe used to slay the couple belonged to Andrew Maggio, he became the police chief's prime suspect in the crime, yet was released after investigators were unable to break down his statement, as well as his account of an unknown man who was supposedly seen lurking near the residence prior to the murders.

The most perplexing aspect of the couple's murder was the creepy writing that was seen on a pavement some distance away from the couple's home. The message written in chalk read: "Mrs. Joseph Maggio will sit up tonight. Just like Mrs. Toney".

These were the first of what a series of bloody attacks that would hold the city of New

Orleans in a stranglehold of terror not seen since Jack the Ripper of London.

Why don't we look at the scene shall we first was this a crime of opportunity maybe but maybe not, because the straight razor that belonged to Andrew Maggio,

How did the killer get it, I have to a couple of theories the first and most logical was that it was in the house and the killer would only use tools that were already in the victim's homes?

The second theory is that the killer stole it from Andrew's barber shop and Andrew only told his employer Esteban Torres that it was having a nick honed from the blade to save from embarrassment from having to admit his tool of the trade stolen and was biding his to either buy a new or when he joined the navy it would not be his problem anymore.

The strangest part is the message on wall and who was Mrs. Toney?

However, later the police speculated that the creepy message on the pavement referred to someone named Tony Schiambra, a lady of Italian descent and one of the large number of grocers who were attacked and slaughtered between 1911 and 1912. Most of those victims had been slain in the same manner i.e. by a man wielding an axe who sneaked into their homes in the dead of night by making small holes in the backdoor. If those earlier crimes were truly connected, the inhumane axeman had been implementing his strategy for quite a while.

Chapter 2

Louis Besumer & Harriet Lowe

In the early hours of June 27, 1918 at the corner of Dorgenois and Laharpe Streets. Louis Besumer and his mistress Harriet Lowe were attacked while sleeping together in bed, Besumer was struck with a hatchet above his right temple, which resulted in a possible skull fracture. Lowe was hacked over the left ear, and found unconscious when police arrived at the scene.

The couple was discovered shortly after 7 AM on the morning of the attack by John Zanca, a driver of a bakery wagon who had come to the grocery in order to make a routine delivery. Zanca found both Besumer and Lowe in a puddle of their own blood, both bleeding from their heads. The axe, which had belonged to Besumer himself, was found in the bathroom of the apartment both Harriet lowe and Louis Besumer were rushed to hospital.

Almost immediately, police arrested potential suspect Lewis Oubicon, a then 41-year-old African American man who had been employed in Besumer's store just a week before the attacks. No evidence existed which could have proved the man guilty, yet police arrested him nonetheless, stating that Oubicon had offered conflicting accounts of his whereabouts on the morning of the attack. Shortly after the attempted murder Lowe stated that she remembered having been attacked by a mulatto man, yet her statement was discounted by police due to her disillusioned state. Robbery was said to be the only possible explanation for the attacks, yet no money or valuables were removed from the couple's home.

Oubicon was later released as police were unable to gather sufficient evidence to hold him accountable for the crimes. Lowe became the centre of a media circus, The Times-Picayune sensationalized Lowe and her outspoken nature upon discovering that she was not the wife of Besumer, but his mistress. A Charity Hospital source discovered the scandal, when Besumer asked to be directed to the room of "Mrs. Harriet Lowe," and was inevitably denied access as no woman by that name was a patient. Besumer's legal wife arrived from Cincinnati in the days immediately following the discovery, which further inflamed the ongoing drama. Lowe further gained media attention as she repeatedly made statements which voiced her dislike of the New Orleans chief of police, as well as her reluctance to comply with police questioning. After the truth of her marital status was revealed publicly, Lowe told reporters from the Times-Picayune that she would no longer aid the police in their investigation, as she suspected that it had been Chief Mooney who first informed the press of the scandal Lowe returned to the home, she shared with Besumer weeks after the attack. One side of her face was partially paralyzed due to the severity of the attack. Lowe died August 5, 1918, just two days after doctors performed surgery in an effort to repair her partially paralyzed face. Just prior to her death, Lowe told authorities that she suspected it was Louis Besumer who had attacked her.

Media attention soon turned to Besumer himself, as a series of letters written in German, Russian, and Yiddish were discovered in a trunk at the man's home. Police suspected that Besumer was a German spy, and government officials began a full investigation of his potential espionage. Weeks later, after going in and out of consciousness, Harriet Lowe told police that she thought Besumer was in fact a German spy, which led to his immediate arrest. Two days later Besumer was released, and two lead investigators of the case were demoted due to unacceptable police work. Besumer was once again arrested in August 1918, after Harriet Lowe, who lay dying in Charity

Hospital after a failed surgery, stated that it was he who had attacked her more than a month previously with his hatchet. He was charged with murder, and served nine months in prison before being acquitted on May 1, 1919, after a ten-minute jury deliberation.

Just one month after the first killings more people are attacked in their home at night but these victims survive the attack even though Harriet Lowe died a little over a month later after a failed procedure to fix her face if she never had the operation she would have lived and Louis Besumer was sent to prison for the crime and as accused of being a spy.

We have two questions about Louis Besumer

1) Was he a spy?

Answer: no, because what self-respecting spy leaves evidence in such and easy to find place like a trunk and why would a spy be a grocer in New Orleans what strategic value does hold to any nation. If he was a spy and his mistress found out it would be easier to murder her quietly and the dump her body in the Mississippi river which wasn't too far from, he lived so if her body was discovered later if she washed further down the river then it would be almost impossible to identify her and because Harriet was his mistress and she disappeared people would not be able to connect him to the disappearance, if he was a spy the state department would have gotten involved and they would have interrogated him.

2) Was he The Axeman?

Definitely not because the attacks continued when he was imprisoned but did he attack Harriet, unlikely because was also attacked but did he hit himself the axe no because he would be either very skilled or very lucky with the weapon to hit himself just hard enough to look bad and not caused serious injury and just have enough time to put the axe bathroom and pass out beside Harriet to be discovered by John Zanca in the morning, so no he was not the attacker.

Most likely Harriet Lowe feeling humiliated upon being discovered having an affair with a married man because back then the community mostly blamed the women for the affair while man was mostly forgiven,

Lowe probably blamed Besumer for her sever injury to her face because she thought he was the main target of the killer.

Chapter 3

Anna Schneider

In the early evening hours of August 5, 1918 on Elmira Street 28-year-old Anna Schneider who was 8 months pregnant awoke to find a dark figure standing over her and was bashed in the face repeatedly. Her scalp had been cut open, and her face was completely covered in blood. Mrs. Schneider was discovered after midnight by her husband, Ed Schneider, who was returning late from work. Schneider claimed that she remembered nothing of the attack, and gave birth to a healthy baby girl two days after the incident. Her husband told police that nothing was stolen from the home, besides six or seven dollars that had been in his wallet. The windows and doors of the apartment appear to have not been forced open, and authorities came to the conclusion that the woman was most likely attacked with a lamp that had been on a nearby table. James Gleason, who police said was an ex-convict, was arrested shortly after Schneider was found. Gleason was later released due to a complete lack of evidence, and stated that he originally ran from authorities because he had so often been arrested. Lead investigators began to publicly speculate that the attack was related to the previous incidents involving Besumer and Maggio.

The attack on Schneider represented a slight change in the Axeman's M.O., she was neither Italian nor a grocer, therefore it now seemed as if anyone in the city could become a target. After another Axeman suspect was cut loose by the police, New Orleans started to fear that some kind of boogeyman was on the loose in their city.

This attacked was very different that Anna Schneider and might not be an Axeman attack because obviously she was not attacked with an axe but with a lamp that was beside the bed also some money was from Ed Schneider wallet but he might have gambled it away and was too ashamed to tell his wife and blamed the assailant and how did intruder gain access to the apartment but this incident did get the authorities to start making connections to the Maggio and Besumer cases.

Chapter 4

Joseph Romano

On August 10, 1918, Pauline and Mary Bruno awoke to the sound of a commotion in the adjoining room where their uncle Joseph Romano who was a grocer resided. Upon entering the room, the sisters discovered that their uncle had taken a serious blow to his head, which resulted in two open cuts. The assailant was fleeing the scene as they arrived, yet the girls were able to distinguish that he was a dark-skinned, heavy-set man, who wore a dark suit and slouched hat. Romano, although seriously injured, was able to walk to the ambulance once it arrived, yet died two days later due to severe head trauma.

The home had been ransacked, yet no items were stolen from Romano. Authorities found a bloody axe in the back yard and discovered that a panel on the back door had been chiselled away. The Romano murder created a state of extreme chaos in the city, with residents living in constant fear of an axeman attack. Police received a slew of reports, in which citizens claimed to have seen an axeman lurking in New Orleans neighbourhoods. A few men even called to report that they had found axes in their back yards.

Joseph Romano was the 3rd person that the Axeman killed but this time Joseph put up a fight and might have died much sooner and there were witnesses to this crime in Joseph's nieces who saw the assailant leaving the scene and the girls gave a description.

Joseph was also a grocer like Joseph Maggio and Louis Besumer is there a connection did the Axeman start his criminal career as a common burglar who thought that had a lot of money the property but discovered he enjoyed violence escalated into murder.

Post the Romano killing, the city of New Orleans went into a gargantuan state of panic fuelled by the media's frenzy that boiled over after murder of Joseph Romano. Media and newspapers began to report on armed vigilantes carrying shotguns who kept a close watch over their families when they slept at night. People began to get rid of their axes. The police were flooded with reports of people claiming that they had seen the axeman moving in their neighbourhoods, placing his axe and chisels outside their lawns while tampering with their doors and windows. One of the numerous reports claimed that the axeman was posing as a woman, and another alleged that he had been found jumping over a fence to escape.

Tremendous fear struck the hearts of people who were determined to keep their families safe and turned panicky. Nevertheless, the force of their panic seemed to have reached the beastly serial killer, as the murders and attacks came to an abrupt halt.

Horrified residents now began to live under constant fear of the mysterious axeman's attack. Their fear worsened when the neither the police nor the investigators could offer any solution to the insane murderer's identity.

Some of the 'heroic' citizens of New Orleans boldly challenged the ruthless mass murderer. Few daredevils (mostly men) submitted editorials to newspapers like the Times-Picayune which dared the Axeman to intrude their homes. One particularly enthusiast even promised 'to leave the window open for him.'

There were numerous mysterious associated with the case that made absolutely no sense whatsoever. For instance, why would the murderous axeman leave the chisel that he used to remove the wooden door panels? Why would he always use the axe present in his victim's place rather than bringing his own? Though majority of the victims he attacked were Italian migrants, some of them weren't, so what was the connection between the victims?

The murderous axeman would usually take a short break from the slaughtering, and would return once again ten months later.

Chapter 5

Charles, Rosie And Mary Cortimiglia

On 10th March 1919, nothing about his way of killing and the type of people he killed changed. This time, his victims were a family of Italian grocers referred to as Cortimiglia's. The mass murderer sneaked into the house of his victims using his trademark chiselling of the backdoor panel, then as usual, he used the axe from the victims' house and stole no money or valuables from the victims' place.

On the corner of Jefferson Avenue and Second Street in Gretna, Louisiana, a New Orleans suburb across the Mississippi River. On the night of March 10, 1919, screams were heard coming from the residence of Charles Cortimiglia, his wife Rosie and their 2-year-old daughter Mary.

Grocer Iorlando Jordano rushed across the street to investigate. Upon his arrival, Jordano noticed that Charles Cortimiglia, his wife, and their daughter had all been attacked by the unknown intruder. Rosie who was attacked alongside her husband, while sleeping with her baby in her arms. She was badly wounded by the axeman stood in the doorway with a serious head wound, clutching her deceased daughter Marty was killed while sleeping in her mother's arms with a single blow to the back of the neck. Charles lay on the floor, bleeding profusely. The couple was rushed to Charity Hospital, where it was discovered that both had suffered skull fractures.

Nothing was stolen from the house, but a panel on the back door had been chiselled away and a bloody axe was found on the back porch of the home. Charles was released two days later, while his wife remained in the care of doctors. Upon gaining full consciousness, Rosie made claims that Iorlando Jordano and his 18-year-old son, Frank, were responsible for the attacks. Iorlando, a 69-year-old man, was in too poor of health to have committed the crimes. Frank Jordano, more than six feet tall and weighing over 200 pounds, would have been too large to have fit through the panel on the back door. Charles Cortimiglia vehemently denied his wife's claims, yet police nonetheless arrested the two and charged them with the murder. The men would later be found guilty. Frank was sentenced to hang, and his father to life in prison. Charles Cortimiglia divorced his wife after the trial. Almost a year later, Rosie announced that she had falsely accused the two out of jealousy and spite. Her statement was the only evidence against the Jordanos, and they were released from jail shortly thereafter.

This attacked was the most tragic because the victim who died was a 2-year-old child which makes the killer even more depraved than ever before, the killer seem also not to be very strong since most if not all his attacks are blitz or when his victims are sleeping.

I wonder how spiteful Rosie Cortimiglia was to accuse Iorlando Jordano and his 18-year-old son, Frank of this terrible crime and almost 2 men's lives were almost destroyed by false allegations.

The Axeman, nevertheless, bears notable infamy and not merely due to the barbarity of his killing. But just like Jack the Ripper and the Zodiac, the mysterious Axeman had written a creepy letter with an odd request.

Chapter 6

A letter from the Axeman

On March 13, 1919, A few days after the attack on the Cortimiglia's, the Axeman decided to write to the Times-Picayune newspaper the letter header said 'Hell'.

Esteemed Mortal:

They have never caught me and they never will. They have never seen me, for I am invisible, even as the ether that surrounds your earth. I am not a human being, but a spirit and a demon from the hottest hell. I am what you Orleanians and your foolish police call the Axeman.

When I see fit, I shall come and claim other victims. I alone know whom they shall be. I shall leave no clue except my bloody axe, besmeared with blood and brains of he whom I have sent below to keep me company.

If you wish you may tell the police to be careful not to rile me. Of course, I am a reasonable spirit. I take no offense at the way they have conducted their investigations in the past. In fact, they have been so utterly stupid as to not only amuse me, but His Satanic Majesty, Francis Josef, etc. But tell them to beware. Let them not try to discover what I am, for it were better that they were never born than to incur the wrath of the Axeman. I don't think there is any need of such a warning, for I feel sure the police will always dodge me, as they have in the past.

They are wise and know how to keep away from all harm.

Undoubtedly, you Orleanians think of me as a most horrible murderer, which I am, but I could be much worse if I wanted to. If I wished, I could pay a visit to your city every night. At will I could slay thousands of your best citizens, for I am in close relationship with the Angel of Death.

Now, to be exact, at 12:15 (earthly time) on next Tuesday night, I am going to pass over New Orleans. In my infinite mercy, I am going to make a little proposition to you people. Here it is: I am very fond of jazz music, and I swear by all the devils in the nether regions that every person shall be spared in whose home a jazz band is in full swing at the time I have just mentioned. If everyone has a jazz band going, well, then, so much the better for you people. One thing is certain and that is that some of your people who do not jazz it out on that specific Tuesday night (if there be any) will get the axe.

Well, as I am cold and crave the warmth of my native Tartarus, and it is about time I leave your earthly home, I will cease my discourse. Hoping that thou wilt publish this, that it may go well with thee, I have been, am and will be the worst spirit that ever existed either in fact or realm of fantasy.

-The Axeman

Saying that he would kill again at 15 minutes past midnight on the night of March 19 but would spare the occupants of any place where a jazz band was playing. That night all of New Orleans' dance halls were filled to capacity, and professional and amateur bands played jazz at parties at hundreds of houses around town. There were no murders that night.

This letter says a lot about the man who wrote it,

It's well written and is very dramatic which would mean that the write is very literate and educated but also probably narcissistic and enjoyed the idea of the whole city being afraid of him and definitely love jazz music.

He most likely had a great time on March 19th with everyone doing what he wanted which probably fed his ego.

At midnight Tuesday evening, 18th March, the residents, along with the revellers of New

Orleans played jazz like they had never done before. All the bars, clubs, and restaurants were buzzing with patrons who wriggled on the music as their lives depended on it. Every musician in town, irrespective of being booked or contracted. Each and every neighbour, family member, friend, stranger had gathered around the jazz maestros, with the bands playing their heart out that evening. All instruments like the saxophone, trumpet, violin, clarinet, piano and the trombone was playing the jazz tune to reach the ears of the axeman. Taking inspiration from the axeman's letter to the Times-Picayune, a composer named Joseph John Davilla claimed that he had composed 'The Mysterious Axeman Jazz (Don't Scare me papa) as he waited for the serial killer. Moreover, on the following Thursday morning, he had placed the sheet of music on sale to the public at a high price. His business plan was so clever that many were forced to think that he could have drafted the letter himself to use the people's fear to his advantage and further sell out his composition.

On St. Joseph's day, March 19th, the Times-Picayune published an illustration that portrayed a family frenziedly playing jazz music on their piano with a look of utmost terror on their innocent faces while waiting for the ruthless axeman to pass over their city. This article illustrated every festivity related to jazz that in that cosmopolitan area and also highlighted the fact that the axeman did not strike that evening. Joseph Davilla later used the illustration as a cover for his renowned, published sheet of music.

Although it's doubtful that every household that night blared out jazz music into the early hours, the Axeman was clearly satisfied with what he heard as not a single attack occurred that night. In fact, the rest of spring and most of the summer would pass before another axe was wielded in terror.

Chapter 7

Steve Boca

On August 10, 1919, another grocer by the name of Steve Boca was attacked whilst he slept, the Axeman cracking his head open with his usual weapon of choice.

Upon regaining consciousness, Boca ran to the street to investigate the intrusion, and found that his head had been cracked open. The grocer ran to the home of his neighbour, Frank Genusa, where he lost consciousness and collapsed.

Nothing had been taken from the home, yet, once again, a panel on the back door of the home had been chiselled away. Boca recovered from his injuries, but could not remember any details of the trauma.

Like most of the other attack the victim was a grocer and Italian were these crimes racially motivated and what was this obsession with grocers, who was this maniac really thinking about when he swung his axe.

Following that attack, a month later on 2nd September, a local druggist known as William Carson, was lucky enough to escape the axe of the deadly axeman when he anxiously fired a number of shots at a trespasser who had broken into his property. The brutal murderer as usual left an axe behind.

Chapter 8

Sarah Laumann

It was the night of September 3, 1919. Neighbours came to check on Sarah Laumann, who had lived alone, and broke into the home when Laumann did not answer. They discovered the 19-year-old lying unconscious on her bed, suffering from a severe head injury and missing several teeth.

The intruder had entered the apartment through an open window, and attacked the woman with a blunt object. A bloody axe was discovered on the front lawn of the building. Laumann recovered from her injuries, yet couldn't recall any details from the attack

However, the attacker came in through the window not the backdoor of Laumann's house, leading some to believe this was not the work of the Axeman but perhaps a copycat.

This attack has a lot in common with the Anna schneider both involved women who were alone asleep in their beds and both managed to survive the attack but why did the intruder use the window instead of the back door like the other break ins.

Chapter 9

Mike Pepitone

It was the night of October 27th 1919 just a few days before Halloween the wife of Italian Grocer Mike Pepitone heard sounds of a struggle coming from the room which her husband resided, Mrs Pepitone entered to a gruesome sight of her husband lying dead on the floor covered in blood in fact the most of the room was splashed with blood including a portrait of the virgin May and two men fleeing.

The mother of six couldn't give an accurate description of the killer. The Pepitone murder was the last of the alleged axeman attacks.

Apart from this additional person, everything else about the event and the crime scene was unchanged from previous Axeman attacks that was it, there were no more axeman attacks afterwards.

Why did the axeman stopped like of famous unsolved serial killings that stop all of a sudden, we may never know?

Everyone has theory of what happened to the Axeman some say he moved away and started again in another state or he died it is a mystery.

Post the murder of the Pepitones, Esther Pepitone along with her children moved to Los Angeles, California. During September the same year, Esther tied the knot with Angelo Albano, whom she had met earlier in New Orleans. Was it purely coincidental, or intentional? Nobody knows, but Albano entered into a business partnership with Joseph Mumfre who was a pharmacist as well as a murderer from New Orleans. Joseph Mumfre had taken the help of numerous aliases and it was rumoured that he was part of a gang that attacked Italian business people. He was a serial offender who had spent time in prison for blowing up an Italian American's grocery shop.

On Mike Pepitone's death anniversary, Mr. Albano left the city to purchase produce. The man seemed to be in a very jovial mood and as per the L.A. Times, eye-witnesses reported that Angelo Albano was humming and whistling joyfully. He reached the grocery store and then the bank, where he made a substantial withdrawal. After that incident, the man disappeared completely, and was never spotted again.

Esther Pepitone, now Mrs. Albano interrogated Mr. Mumfre about her husband's whereabouts. Mumfre provided her with everything he knew that her husband had been abducted and warned her upfront that she would be asked for money.

On 5th December 1924, Joe Mumfre paid a visit to the Albano House and did as what he had warned Esther. When Esther Albano answered the door, Mumfre claimed to have a gun with him and threatened her to give all of her money and jewellery to him. The cunning lady pretended to oblige but she took out a 0.38 gun and fired all the shots into his chest and head. She then retrieved another gun and unloaded that too into his dead body out of sheer fury and anxiety. The local public officer reported the cause of death to be gunshot wounds to his chest, abdomen and head. However, he couldn't explain the reason for the murder; out of self-defence or purely a murder intention on Esther Albano's part. And when the police interrogated her and demanded the reason for the killing she claimed that Joe Mumfre had murdered her husband. But the truth was her husband Mike Pepitone was already dead while her second husband Angelo Albano was merely missing. Eventually, she was tried and convicted of her hand in his disappearance as well as Joseph Mumfre's murder. Till date, nobody knows what happened to her husband.

Suspects

There were some theories about the identity of the murderous axeman. Since majority of the serial killer's victims were either Italian Americans or Italian immigrants, people presumed that it was supposedly a sort of hate crime or a series of hate crimes. Nevertheless, with each unresolved case of serial killing, people also alleged that there was no axeman involved. Rather, they stated that other men took the axeman's onslaught as inspiration and took the mantle on and became the next axemen.

Now the axeman wasn't a demon or satanic spirit as he claimed to be, although a number of theories emerged which suggested that he was indeed a supernatural force. Nonetheless, many of the people agreed that the ruthless serial killer was merely a man. But who could the axeman possibly be? Well, there are quite a number of men who fell under the radar.

Suspect 1: The Black Hand

Since the majority of the Axeman's attacks were on Italian-American grocers, it has led some to believe that they were all victims of an early form of Mafia, called the Black Hand. Black Hand crime was a name given to an extortion method used in Italian neighbourhoods at this time, therefore the murders could be linked to unpaid extortion debts. However, the Axeman frequently left suspects alive, which many Mafia experts believe would not have been the case if they'd have been true Black Hand attacks.

In a similar vein, many Sicilian immigrants to American at that time had a deep distrust of the authorities, which led them to take disputes into their own hands and settle them the old-fashioned way, otherwise known as the 'vendetta'. The vendetta could well have been the reason behind a number of the attacks.

Suspect 2: Joseph Mumfre

Famous crime writer by the name of Colin Wilson postulates that Joseph Mumfre could have been the infamously murderous axeman. Mumfre is the only legitimate suspect to have ever been linked to the real identity of the Axeman. Mumfre led a blackmailing gang in New Orleans that targeted Italian Americans.

In December 1920, a year after the Axeman had struck his last victim Mike Pepitone, Mumfre himself was shot dead by the widow of Pepitone in Los Angeles. Mrs Pepitone claimed Mumfre was the Axeman and remembered seeing him run from the bedroom the night her husband was killed.

Mumfre had served time in prison, the dates apparently coinciding between 1912 and 1918 when the Axeman attacks stopped. They resumed at the same time Mumfre was a free man. He left New Orleans after the killing of Mike Pepitone, again explaining why the Axeman seemingly disappeared after 1919.

However, recent research carried out by another famous crime writer named Michael Newton inside police records, reports along with newspaper archives into the period has failed to find any evidence of a man named

Joseph Mumfre being attacked and killed in New Orleans, leading some to believe his existence as purely an urban legend.

Moreover, Michael Newton was unable to find any information about Mrs. Pepitone, who was also referred to as Esther Albano in few sources while in others she was merely known as 'woman who alleged to be Pepitone's widow'. He couldn't find any sources which stated that she was convicted, arrested or tried for any such crime. In addition to that, it wasn't even known that she had even been in California at that time. According to Newton, the surname 'Momfre' was not an uncommon name in New Orleans during the period when the crimes took place. It seems that there was indeed a possibility that a man by the name of Joseph Mumfre existed in New Orleans with a criminal history and who might have been associated with organized crime. Unfortunately, local records during that period aren't substantial enough for giving confirmation to this sort of info or even to identify the person. Colin's Wilson's information is nothing more than a myth and currently there is no further proof on the killer's identity then there was at that time.

The Italian couple called Schiambra, who were some of the early victims of the axeman were gunned down by a trespasser in their home in the early morning of 16th May. The husband survived but the wife wasn't that lucky. As per the newspapers, the main suspect is referred to by the name 'Mumfre' a number of times. Despite, Mumfre's style of killing was quite different from the actual axeman's, if he was truly the axeman, the

Schiambra family were very likely to have been early targets of the serial killer.

As per the scholar named Richard Warner, the prime suspect in the killings was Frank 'Doc' Mumfrey aka Leon Joseph Monfre.

Suspect 3: Copycat Killers

Although the Axeman had a very distinct M.O., not all of the killings followed it to the letter, leading some to believe the Axeman was, in fact, several people who may or may not have been working together to terrorise the community.

Suspect 4: Ungodly Demon

His ability to appear in people's houses in the middle of the night and vanish just as easily, have some believing the Axeman was indeed what he said he was in his letter to the press -

'the worst spirit that ever existed either in fact or realm of fancy.'

A professor of journalism and communication named Dirk Gibson at the University of New Mexico, who specialises in murder stated that a dozen men and women were attacked with an axe between 1918 and1919 in New Orleans. Majority of them were Italian grocers who were killed with their own axes. But, the Times-Picayune Newspaper portrayed these killings as fantastical and supernatural stories thus, tapping into people's fear of the occult and striking terror into the hearts of the people. A curator emeritus of the Hogan Jazz Archive at Tulane University named Bryce Raeburn also says that the letter by the supposed killer called the 'axeman', could have only worked in New Orleans wherein, after the civil war, the massive plantations had been broken down post the North's victory and a dozen Black Americans rushed into the city to live alongside the whites, Jewish and others. Hence, the latest music of that era and place called the Jazz became of a reflection of the multi-racial experience. Raeburn stated that Jazz music was breaking all barriers of segregation that was meant to separate the people.

So it has been theorised that perhaps the axeman was gaining revenge against Italian Immigrants and Italian Americans since the African American Jazz musicians weren't receiving the credit they deserved. In 1917, the very first Jazz recording was conducted by an Italian Immigrant by the name of Nick LaRocca, as stated by Eric Hofbauer who is a jazz composer and guitarist who has an affiliation with the faculty at Emerson College and the Longy School of Music of Bard College.

Eric Hofbauer stated that it was a highly controversial record in the history of Jazz as there was no improvisation. The music was similar to jazz, but NOT jazz. However, many of them including Nick LaRocca stated that he and his band called 'The Original Dixieland Jazz Band had invented Jazz.

So, the most obvious question that arises in people's minds is, was the serial killer called the axeman trying to get revenge from the Italian-American band for stealing credit? Maybe not, Hobauer claimed. Eric Hofbauer put forward another theory that the axeman was furious about the shutting down of the red light district, Storyville, in New Orleans in 1917. The Navy closed down all public places where jazz prevailed in the neighbourhood-

brothels, gambling dens, dance halls, clubs etc.

Or perhaps, the mass murderer was trying to save jazz's honour? During the summer of 1918, the Times-Picayune had posted an article that rebuked jazz and wrote insulting comments on it such as, jazz being nothing but noise and not music. Another theory was that the serial killer was merely a psychotic, yet, greatest marketer of jazz in the entire nation.

Hofbauer stated that the night when the entire New Orleans played the jazz out of fear from the axeman's attack, every jazz band in the city was performing, either at a club, bar, a dance hall or a home. So, the serial killer's main motivation was perhaps to help the jazz musicians get paid that year.

So, axeman was considered a hero in terms of style but mocked and rebuked for his thought process i.e., committing mass murders just to promote jazz and its musicians.

Miriam Davis, the renowned author of 'The Axeman of New Orleans: The True Story," put forward her own thoughts on the matter. She believed that the eerie letter couldn't have possibly been written by the Axeman. She alleged that the axeman was assuredly not a well-educated man and rather a working class person. Probably a burglar. According to her, the person who had written the letter was most likely a well-educated man and not a petty commoner. Moreover, she disregarded that theory of Joseph Mumfre being the axeman as she claimed that Mumfre was in prison when majority of the crimes took place in New Orleans. Nevertheless, she did have few intriguing theories on the serial killers victims, who were, mostly either Italian-Americans pr Italian migrants. She postulated that most of the Italian migrants present in New Orleans at that time were from Sicily and possessed very dark skin. As a result, they didn't fit into either the black or white categories and so, they were ready to take up jobs that whites refused to do. Thus, they performed quite well economically.

Furthermore, Davis was suspicious of some sort of ethnic or racial anxiety inside the brutal serial killer as they believed that the no-so-white looking foreigners were doing better than what he thought his people ought to be doing. In addition to that, Davis believed that a man by the name of John Joseph Devila had written that letter. Devila was a jazz composer and musician and post the publishing of the letter, he had come out with the composition called, 'The Mysterious Axeman's Jazz (Don't Scare me Papa). So according to Davis, the jazz man made a fortune off that song and so, she considered him to be a likely suspect for the letter.

Davis made another suggestion to the public that to try and avoid irrational fear, they should get a huge dog who would bark in the middle of the night if anyone attempted to trespass their property.

Connection to Tacoma

During early 1947, the police captured a forty-five-year-old African-American transient named Jake Bird suspected of jumping trains across the country. He made a confession that he had killed a couple in Tacoma, however, the New Orleans Police Department picked on him as a suspect for the axe murders of 1918. During interrogation, the man confessed that he had murdered forty-four people across the country. However, the most obvious link that connected Bird to the axeman was that he used to reside in New Orleans during the serial killer's reign of terror in 1918. Moreover, he was a growing teen during that time and so, he could easily fit through small holes that the axeman made in the door panels. Nevertheless, nothing else linked Bird to those brutal crimes in New Orleans, police presumed that his confession was a false one. But he was found guilty of the murders in Tacoma and was sentenced to death. When his punishment was declared, Bird made a prediction that every soul present in the courtroom would die before he did. Call it coincidence or the result of a curse, but six of the court members did face death before Washington State hanged him on 15th July 1949.

Afterward

And just like that, it was all over. The Axeman was never seen or heard of again, like the spirit he claimed to be, he simply vanished into thin air. The true identity of the killer would remain one crime's greatest unsolved mysteries.

Nevertheless, the brutal axeman's reign of terror across New Orleans has been immortalised through various books, movies, TV series, television programs, podcasts as well as numerous modern virtual reality games, that have preserved the mass murderers bloody legacy in some way or another.

In 1919, local tune writer Joseph John Davilla wrote the song, "The Mysterious Axman's Jazz (Don't Scare Me Papa)". Published by

New Orleans based World's Music Publishing Company, the cover depicted a family playing music with frightened looks on their faces.

The 1945 book Gumbo Ya-Ya, A Collection of Louisiana Folk Tales includes a chapter on the Axeman entitled "Axeman's Jazz", which helped spark renewed interest in the murders. The book also reproduced the cover of the 1919 sheet music.

An Australian rock band referred to as the 'Beasts of Bourbon' released an album in 1984 titled 'The Axeman Jazz'.

A renowned writer by the name of Julie Smith adapted a fictional version of the Axeman incidents in her novel called 'The Axeman's Jazz' released in 1991.

The Axeman's incidents and killing spree have also been referred to in the short story of

Poppy Z. Brite called 'Mussolini and the Axeman's Jazz' that was published in 1997.

The Axeman has also found its place in Sister Vigilante's short story in Chuck Palahnuik's novel called Haunted, released in 2005.

The famous song, 'Deathjazz' by the famous Los Angeles-based rock band, One Ton Project narrates the story of the Axeman. In addition to that, Fila Brazillia's song 'Tunstall and Californian Haddock contains a sentence from the Axeman's letter to the Times-Picayune at the beginning.

Las Vegas based band named One Ton Project, narrates the story of the axeman.

In addition to that, Fila Brazillia's song 'Tunstall and Californian Haddock contains a sentence from the Axeman's letter to the Times-Picayune at the beginning.

The 2012 novel titled Red, White and Blood by Christopher Farnsworth is based on a lethal spirit referred to as the Boogeyman, which has possessed endless bodies through various stages of history, that includes the Axeman of New Orleans.

The 2014 novel titled; The Axeman's Jazz by Ray Celestin has been adapted fictionally from the Axeman of New Orleans's case.

In the popular T.V. series, American Horror Story: Coven, has an episode titled 'The Axeman Cometh' in which the serial killer is played by Danny Huston. Moreover, the Axeman has also been depicted in Season 3-6 of another hit television series titled, 'The Originals'.

The Axeman has been depicted in Hildred Rex's short story titled, A Slinking Agent of the Devil (at 3AM). And also the serial killer's story has been covered in Opus 1 of the dark fictional anthology called The Egg.

A true crime podcast called 'My Favorite Murder covered the Axeman's tale on their sixtieth episode titled 'Jazz it'. Another popular podcast on true crimes in America called Unsolved Murders conducted a 3-part mini-series on the Axeman of New Orleans which concluded with the hosts' opinions of who they believed to be responsible for his heinous crimes.

Another well-known series called 'Stuff You Missed in History Class took up a two-part mini-series based on the axeman in which they played with the concept of his hideous acts and killings. In addition to that, a paranormal and true crime podcast called And That's Why We Drink, conducted an episode on the Axeman's topic on it's thirty-ninth episode titled, 'A Girl Named German and La La Land 1 1/2'

On 13th, Eisregen, a German black/death metal band formed in 1995, released the hit song 'Axtmann' which narrates the story of his inhumane crimes.

A YouTube series called Buzz Feed that dwells deep into unsolved true crime stories, cases as well as supernatural beings, delved into the numerous theories and stories with regards to the Axeman in their 1st Episode of Season 1 titled, The Terrifying Axeman of New Orleans.

The famous author and historian, Alan G. Gauthreaux depicted a complete profile of the brutal serial killer called the Axeman in his book titled, Italian Lousiana: History, heritage and Tradition released in 2014.

The entertaining news satire program, Last week Tonight with John Oliver, talked about the Axeman during the 13th episode of season 6 called Medical Devices. In the enlightening episode, Oliver gave a brief history of the mass murderer after displaying the DePuy sales team celebrating their successful number of hip devices sold. The celebration was based on the theme Mardi Gras, and involved a man disguised as the dreaded axeman.

Another American Jazz Band known as the Squirrel Nut Zippers, released a song called 'Axeman Jazz (Don't Scare Me Papa)" in their album released in 2018 called "Beasts of Burgundy"

In the world-famous Video Game enjoyed by millions of youngsters across the world, The Waking Dead: Saints and Sinners, you can find a dozen references. One of the characters in the game indicates him in his dialogue and a special axe can be discovered inside a safe with the words, 'the axeman cometh' written on the side. In addition to that, there is a reference to the character liking jazz along with the axeman's famous quote from his eerie letter that has been used to describe the special axe to be found, referred to as the Esteemed Mortal.

Today, the brutal Axeman of New Orleans isn't a well-known mass murderer when compared to his various counterparts like Jack the ripper, Jeffrey Dahmer, Harold Shipman, John Wayne Gacy, H.H Holmes, Pedro Lopez, as well as Ted Bundy. Nonetheless, as any legend does, he continues tormenting the citizens of New Orleans. He is both legend and ghost. Who knows, you may get a chance to meet him, on a ghostly tour of his local hauntings. However, the brutal axeman that was once horribly feared, has become the stuff of legends and tales of boogeyman narrated around campfires. And to add salt to wound, his victims didn't receive justice. The terrorising Axeman's legacy would go on to be remembered to this day.

Recently, a creepypasta (horror related legend shared across the internet) which is written by an anonymous editor at a publishing company claims to be in possession of a picture of the axeman fleeing a crime scene at night. It's nothing but a creepypasta so just consider it for what it is worth.